The Big Book of Herbal Medicine 2 books in 1

Herbal Remedies for Children & How to Be an Herbalist

Amayeta Shan

HERBAL REMEDIES FOR CHILDREN

INTRODUCTION

Herbal remedies for children are often used to treat various ailments, including cold and flu symptoms, rashes on the skin, digestion problems, and stomachaches. However, such treatments are not always safe because they can be made from plant leaves or flowers and may contain toxicsubstances.

The following is an introduction to herbalremedies for children. This book describes what herbal remedies are, the types of herbs that can be used for different illnesses, the scientific evidence about their effectiveness and possible side effects, and sources for all this information.

Herbal remedies for children are made from plantleaves and flowers, which have been dried and crushed into a powder. Sometimes people useother plantmaterials such as bark, roots, seeds, andfruits in many traditional medicines. Most herbal remedies are based on well-known herbs such as echinacea, St. John's wort, garlic, Ginkgo Biloba, ginseng, and kava. But a wide variety of herbal remedies is also made from lesser-known plants such as mallow,cleavers, and geraniums.

Mothers often use herbal remedies to providesome treatment to their children, usually while they are recovering from illness. Also, many practitioners use herbal treatment to complementconventional medicine and are not necessarily associated with tradition or religion. Many people whouse herbal remedies for upbringing and health maintenance have no training in herbalmedicine. These people may buy herbs in health food stores or pharmacies without consulting a trained herbalist.

Herbal remedies for children should not be used on sick babies and infants because the herbs mightinterfere with their natural healing ability. Herbs that should never be given to children includeephedra, ma huang, chaparral, and comfrey. Because of its toxicity, the FDA has prohibited these herbs as they are known to cause liver damage, cardiovascular problems, and allergies. Inaddition, comfrey has been linked to several adverse side effects, including liver damage, gastrointestinal problems, and skin irritations.

The following is an introduction to herbal remedies for children. These are often used for colds and flu because they contain immune-stimulating properties. They are also helpful ifa child has an allergy or asthma because herbs can soothe the inflammation caused by them. For example, an herbal formula called "Goldenrod" contains echinacea, elderflower, Oregon grape root, thyme, peppermint, and licorice. It is often used to treat colds in children.

Herbal remedies for children are commonly used for digestive problems such as indigestion, diarrhea, and constipation. Chamomile tea, a soother of the gastrointestinal tract, can be given to infants to help them sleep if they are colicky. Fenugreek is said to alleviate chronic diarrhea. Peppermint and chamomile teas can calm stomachcramps.

Table of Content:

MEDICINAL PLANTS AND THEIRUSES FOR CHILDREN

Trying out medical plants wouldn't be bad for seeing your children fit and healthy. Plants not only draw you closer to nature, but someplants will act as medicine.

The Health Benefits of Lavender

Besides its aroma, you can use lavender tea to give your children a goodsleep at night. For children's massage, you can use lavender oil, whichis also profitable for aromatherapy and hair treatment. There are numerous advantages to having this plant in your home.

The health benefits of lavender:

- It helps to free a child's tension, and their minds

- will become stress-free due to its use.

- It can relieve migraine or headaches.

- Also, you can use the essential oil of lavender

- in a diffuser.

- It can relieve relentlesspain in children.

- Lavender helps to treat respiratory problem

- sin children.

- It supports sleep in children.

- You can use it in several treatments for healthy

    hair and skin (for children).

The Health Benefits of Aloe Vera

Are you aware the herbal name of this plant is Aloe Vera, and its family is Liliaceae? I believe thisis a powerful plant every parent should grow in their homes. I cannot deny the great uses of AloeVera. This beautiful plant will help you to soothe sunburn and heal wounds. Globally, this plant is grown in tropical weather. You will treasure knowing how good this plant is. The health benefits of aloe vera:

Are you aware heartburn is linked to digestive disorders? You can solve the heartburn issues of your children with aloe vera. Because of its low toxicity, this plant can be used as a therapy.

- Aloe vera gel preserves the fruits and vegetables fresh and blocks the growth of unhealthy bacteria on them.

- The good news is that it can be used as a mouthwash (because ithasVitamin C), which helps fightplaque.

- You can also reduce the blood sugar level (in children) by giving them one or two tablespoons of Aloe Vera juice daily.

The Health Benefits of Lemon Balm

Are you aware that the herbal name of lemon balmis Melissa officinalis? It isa perfect medicinal plantto lessen anxiety and stress in adult children. Anxiety and stress block children's lives because they cannot lead a healthy activity with high anxiety and fear.

The bad news is that their body will not function accurately if their mind is troubled. But on the other hand, the lemon plant's taste is delightful and rich, and you can use it in dishes like ice cream,teas, and more for children. As forfear, it works well, so lemon balm is used to soothe nervous youngsters. It also helps to ward off insects from your home.

The health benefits of lemon balm:

As highlighted above, LEMON BALM reduces children's restlessness, stress,and anxiety.

- It assists in reducing swelling in children.

- The most conventional use oflemon balm is that it can comfortably treat cold sores in children.

The Health Benefits of Neem

The great news is that neem has been used as a

therapeutic herb for over 2000 years. Regularly it is used to kill bacteria that cause infection in children. When you know the advantages of neem trees, you will be astonished to see how nature holds the cure. The unique gift is that Neem seeds are used to extract neem oil, which has therapeutic qualities, andit becomes the mainpart of makeup and beauty products like hair oil, soaps, and face wash in the home.

Besides, the neem plant's flowers are white and frail. So you can also cook ordry roast and sprinklethem on many meals for garnishing.

The health benefits of neem:

- diseases and defend their bodies from The paste of neem leaves

- will assist heal thechildren's worms andinsect bites.

- It will aid in treating children's acne and

- reducing dark spots ontheir skin.

- The Neem leaf and honey paste will assistin treating air boil inchildren.

- It will help combat diseases like ringworms, eczema, itching, andother mild skin ailments.

- This plant will boost your children's immune systems.

Lastly, you can boil some leaves in water and let the water cool. Now youcan use it to wash the children's eyes if they have any irritation, tiredness,or redness in their eyes.

The Health Benefits of Thyme

This herb is known for cooking, but you can also use it as a mouthwash. The great advantage is thatit has antifungal and antibacterial features, makingit distinct from other plants for your children. It can also prevent the children from contracting anyinfection that can make them sick.

The health benefits of thyme:

- It helps to treat cough and sore throats in children.

- It helps to improve blood circulation in the body of children and treats breathing difficulties.

- It helps develop a competent immune system(in children).

- Due to the residence of thymol, it can be used as a mouthwash andvapor rub for children.

The Health Benefits of Marigold

Do you know many people grow Marigold because it has fragrant flowers? Still, you can takeadvantage of improving the children's skin healthcondition by using these flowers as they contain many antioxidants and healthy composites. Theother benefit of these plants is that it helps to keepinsects away from home.

The health benefits of marigold:

- It helps to treat skin diseases in children.

- It helps to reduce (swelling) inflammation in children.

- It is also advantageous to treat ear pain or infection in children.

- This plant's flowers havepowerful antibacterial and antiseptic characteristics, which give it a notable place among other plants.

The Health Benefits of Garlic

Most people use garlic in cooking, but this super plant helps you fight infections and diseases. Iwould advise all parents to embrace this super herb!The most significant benefit you get is that itwill help maintain the children'sbody cholesterol. It would help if you allowed your children to eat garlic frequently for a healthy body. Allowing

them (the children) to eat raw garlic will be more advantageous than cooked garlic.

The health benefits of garlic:

- It maintains cholesterol levels in your body

(most especially the children). In this way, it will prevent them from having heartdisease.

- Besides, reducing cholesterol levels inchildren will also help maintain blood pressure.

- It works well to fight many infections and diseases in children and improves theirdigestive functions.

- It will increase the flavor of your dishes ifyou add it to your meals.

The Health Benefits of Peppermint

Do you know the famous peppermint is a common herb you taste in gum, desserts, or even your toothpaste? The good news is that peppermint will help soothe and relieve tummy aches, nausea, and muscle pain in children. The health benefits of peppermint:

- It helps to alleviate allergies andheadaches in children.

- It assists in improving your digestive system and manages bad breath in children because it is extremely antibacterial.

- No one can reject its effectiveness in lessening nausea, gas, andindigestion.

The Health Benefits of Parsley

If you don't know, now you will know! Parsley is used for garnishing your tasty dishes, and at the same time, it will help improve the children's immune system. Besides this, it is alsoimmeasurable for the bone and digestive healthofthe children. In addition, it carries high

concentrations of vitamin K, antioxidants, and other composites. All these things join collectivelyto make this herb exceptional for children.

The health benefits of parsley:

- It fights bad breath on children.

- Parsley is a rich source of antioxidants.

- You can create a juice or brew tea from this herb for your children.

- It can support digestive health (children) and be suitablefor bones.

The Health Benefits of Rosemary

Rosemary is high in vitamins and minerals and aids in the proper functioning of children's bodies. It can enhance children's memory and support theirhair growth. Rosemary tea is very useful for a childstruggling with hair loss.

The health benefits of rosemary:

- It helps to enhance blood circulation in children and reducesinflammation too.

- Rosemary treats children's bad breath and supports liver health.

- It helps improve children's memory, enhancing overall brainfunction.

OTHER MEDICINAL PLANTS

Herbs usually work by increasing or decreasing thenumber of certain chemicals in the body. These chemicals include hormones, nerve signals, and cellular messengers involved in the functioning ofyour body. Herbs can also be used to improve a person's mood or help them to relax. Different types of herbs can do this, and they can be prepared in many ways. The following information will go over some of the most commonones and what they may be used for.

St. John's Wort

What is it made from?

The entire herb is used as a remedy. It can be usedas a tincture by itself or in combination with otherherbs.

What does it do for your child?

St. John's wort treats depression and anxiety disorders, including post-traumatic stress disorder (PTSD).

How should my child take it?

The dosage of St. John's wort will depend on the situation and what it is supposed to help with. Fordepression, up to 900 mg per day of an extract standardized at 0.3% hypericin. Up to 600 mg perday of an extract standardized at 0.3% hypericin may be used for anxiety. For PTSD, 300 mg takenthree times per day for up to eight weeks has beenused.

Valerian

What is it made from?

The entire herb is used as a remedy. It can be takenas a tincture, capsule, or tablet.

What does it do for your child?

Valerian is used for sleep disorders and insomnia because it affects certain sleep-related chemicals.

How should my child take it?

The dosage of valerian will depend on the situation and what it is supposed tohelp with. Forsleep disorders and insomnia, up to 40 drops of anoil tincture (1:5) taken three times per day may beused.

Yarrow

What is it made from?

The entire herb is used as a remedy. It can be takenas a tincture, capsule, or tablet.

What does it do for your child?

Yarrow is used in shingles, fever, frostbite, and

some types of arthritis. It may also help with muscle spasms and cramps because it influences certain body chemicals associated with muscle contractions.

How should my child take it?

The dosage of Yarrow will depend on the situationand what it is supposed to help with. For example,for shingles, fever, frostbite, and some types of arthritis, 1-2 ml of an oil tincture (1:5) 3 times perday. In addition, 2-3 drops of an oil tincture (1:5) taken three times per day may be used for musclespasms and cramps.

Stickseed

What is it made from?

The entire herb is used as a remedy. It can be taken as a tincture or tea.What does it do for your child?

Stickseed is used with arthritis and rheumatism because it influences certain substances in the body involved with pain.

How should my child take it?

The dosage of stickseed will depend on the situation and what it is supposed to help with. Forexample, for arthritis and rheumatism, 1-2 ml of an oil tincture (1:5) taken three times per day maybe used.

Plantain

What is it made from?

The entire plant is used as a remedy. It can be taken as a tea by itself or incombination withother herbs.

What does it do for your child?

Plantain is used to reduce diarrhea because it affects fluids in the body.How should my childtake it?

10-20 drops of an oil tincture (1:8) taken up tothree times per day may beused.

Calendula

What is it made from?

The entire herb is used as a remedy. It can be taken as a tea or capsule, either by itself or in combination with other herbs.

What does it do for your child?

Calendula is used to heal wounds and skin infections because it affectscertain chemicals in the body involved with healing.

How should my child take it?

The dosage of calendula will depend on the situation and what it is supposed to help with. Forexample, 3-10 drops of an oil tincture (1:5) taken daily may be used for wounds and skin infections.

Eyebright
What is it made from?

The entire herb is used as a remedy. It can be taken as a tea or capsule, either by itself or in combination with other herbs.

What does it do for your child?

Eyebright treats conjunctivitis and cosmetic conditions like dark circles underthe eyes becauseit affects specific compounds involved with your eyesight and eye health.

How should my child take it?

The dosage of eyebright will depend on the situation and what it is supposed to help with. For example, 3-10 drops of an oil tincture (1:5) taken three times per day may be used for conjunctivitis.

Passionflower
What is it made from?

The entire herb is used as a remedy. It can be taken as a tea or capsule, either by itself or in combination with other herbs.

What does it do for your child?

Passionflower improves sleep because it influences certain body chemicalsassociated with sleep cycles.

How should my child take it?

The dosage of passionflower will depend on the situation and what it is supposed to help with. Forexample, 3-10 drops of an oil tincture (1:5) taken three times per day may be used for sleep disorders.

Check the Use of Medicinal Herbs With YourPhysician

If you want to cure your child of a particular illness, herbs are not all they arecracked up to be. Misusing them and taking too many at once can affect your child's immune system and cause problems like respiratory troubles anddiarrhea. Asa result, many parents prefer their child's grandparents or other close family members to give them herbal remedies instead of doctors.

If you try these, be sure to tell your child's doctor.If your child takes a prescription medicine withoutthe doctor's concern, it could risk serious side effects. It could also lead to a quick death if the two medications interfere.

Most of the time, the above herbs are used for headaches and other minor pains in addition to your child's regular medications. They can help relieve some symptoms and make their overall experience more bearable. But if you notice any changes or your child gets sicker, one or two of these herbs may not be enough, and you should contact to check out by a medical professional immediately.

TEN NATURAL REMEDIES FOR KIDS

Do you know when you become a parent, it's imperative to have a stockpile of things on hand? Your kid falls, gets a scrape while playing, has a fever or discomfort, touches something extremely hot (like a pot or the oven), gets a nasty sore, or requires an immune system boost. The list can go on and on. It would be helpful if you had an arsenal of natural treatments.

Presumably, you have a box of medications or a first aid kit full of useful items, but did you know that your home can act as your medicine cabinet? It can do double duty as a treatment for all kinds of common illnesses or ailments. Plus, experimental studies back up some of these homeremedies. First, however, take your child to the doctor as soon as possible for ongoing problems.

Supplements and Homemade Hand Sanitizer

+

Immune Building Herbs for Kids

Do you know it's necessary to keep your kid's immune system running high during the cold andflu season? You should also know that having your children wash their hands constantly is essential, especially during this pandemic. Here are remarkable herbs and supplements that are potent immune-builders and a do-it-yourself recipe for hand sanitizer that yourchildren can use.

Immune-building herbs and supplements

- Elderberry

- Echinacea

- Goldenseal

- Vitamin C

- Vitamin D

- Oregano oil

- Black seed oil

- Hand sanitizer

Do you know how to make an exceptional recipe for a strong hand sanitizer? Instead of rubbing alcohol on your kid's hands (which is not as perfect), why not try making yours?

Recipe type:

Homemade hand sanitizer
Ingredients:

- 3 oz. high-proof vodka

- 1 oz. pure aloe vera gel

- 5-10 drops of lavender essential oil

- 30 drops tea tree essential oil

- ¼ teaspoon vitamin E oil

Instructions:

1. Pour the essential oils into a small glass container. Then mix it all.

2. Add alcohol and remix it.

3. Then add aloe vera gel, and shake properly

4. Shake the mixture tenderly before using it!

Kids With Sleep Issues and Sleep Apnea

Do you know Kids can and do get sleep apnea? The symptoms can include:

- They snore most nights loudly.

- They can stop breathing and snort, gasp for air, and pause in their breathing.

- Sweat massively during their sleep.

- They sleep in unusual positions.

- Most of the night was spent restlessly.

It can add to daytime tiredness and behavioralproblems at school when undiagnosed and not

treated quickly. Recent research found that kids who snore aloud were twice as likely to haveeducation predicaments.

To make it worse, when kids experience a night ofpoor sleep, they are more likely to be hyperactive,have trouble paying attention, and show symptoms of attention deficit disorder. Sleep apnea in children may also be connected with slowed growth and cardiovascular problems.

If your kid has sleep apnea, be on the lookout forsome of these signs:

- Trouble waking up in the morning.

- Have headaches in the morning and throughout the day.

- They are sensitive, irritable, hostile, and experience distress.

- Problems with behavior or social interaction at school or home.

- The kid has a nasal voice and breathes heavily through their mouth.

Using CPAP Mask

The principal thing to do is get your kid to a specialist and have them tested. Your kid may need their tonsils removed immediately, or other items may be blocking their airways. The specialist can also order a child-size mask to wear at night called CPAP (continuous positive airway pressure device).

Try and Learn the Didgeridoo

I get it; this isn't something you've got resting around the home. You may nothave heard of it either, but if your child suffers from sleep apnea, this bizarre wind instrument called aDidgeridoo might help in the short term.

According to recent studies, 4-months of playing the didgeridooworked well for modest sleep apnea patients, which gave thema better night's sleep and decreased daytime drowsiness. But, youmay ask, how does it work? First, you should know that playingthe instrument will empower your child by strengthening the upper airway and preventing it from narrowing as the child

inhales. Hey! You should know that going the extramile to learn to play a musical instrument to help with breathing and lung ability has been used for kids and grown-ups for several ages.

Petroleum Jelly and Listerine for Sores (Bliss)

Do you know that sores (blisters) hurt and can cause distress to your kid?

Do you need a fast remedy?

Listerine is as great as a breath freshener and an antiseptic, but Listerine can also dry out sores yourchildren may have.

Apply the antiseptic to your child's sores (blisters)twice daily using a cotton ball until the sores dry up and the pain disappears. Furthermore, a recentstudy suggests utilizing petroleum jelly ona sore (blister) for short painrelief. The great news is that Listerine has been used for several years as a straightforward way to treat sores (blisters). So if your kid has a blister, this commonremedy works perfectly!

Lemon Balm for Cold Sores

It's no more news that lemon balm is one of the most effective remedies. Young adults and younger children can get severe cold sores. They're prompted by the HSV (Herpes simplex virus) thatpenetrates tissues in the body when a kid is growing; it lies dormant and can emerge later in life as a teen.

Sometimes cold sores are a result of:

- Too much exposition to sunlight.

- Respiratory diseases.

- Emotional strain.

It's high in polyphenols, which have antiviral properties, and tastes and smells delicious. A recent study found that once healed with lemon balm, not a single cold sore recurrence happened.Try lemon balm salve; it can also be used for chapped lips, cuts, minor burns, scrapes, and much more.

Using Ginger for Motion Sickness

Are you going on a journey with your kids? First, you'll need the most sorted- after herb, ginger!Ginger tea, pills, or syrup! They all work for motion sickness or if your child feels unstable.

As a hint, you should know ginger is one of thoseremedies you want to keep in your pocket, kitchen,or even your home first-aid bag. When taking yourkids on a journey, you should take ginger pills formotion illnesses that mightpop up along the way. If you want to use it with essential oils, then rub the ginger oil on the soles of your kid's feet for fastrelief.

One research found that ginger worked best for motion sickness than anti- nausea medicine. Also, it was found that ginger helped with seasickness.

Using a Duct Tape for Warts

I know this is shocking, but I can confirm itworks magic! Do you knowusing duct tape to eliminate warts is a myth? Nevertheless, it serves and does a greater job than freezing them off. In a recent study, duct tape got rid ofover 80 percent of warts in less than three months.

This is how to use it on your children's warts:

- You should make sure the wart and surrounding skin are clean andneat.

- Then cut a piece of duct tape bigger than the wart and press itintothe spot.

- Remove the tape every 3-days, rub the wart with a sandpaper boardor pumice stone, and redoit until the wart is gone.

Banana Peel for Warts (And so Much More)

Do you know if you don't have duct tape closeby for that annoying wart,then you can try usinga very ripe banana peel? To get started, you rub theinside of the peel on the child's wart a little every day.

Bananas can also assist with the following. Massage a banana peel (the inner portion of the banana) on an irritation caused by an insect bite or poison ivy to reduce swelling and relieve discomfort.

Furthermore, it will help if you know banana peelalso has anti-acne qualities.To get anti-microbial and anti-inflammatory effects, massage the inner portion of the peel over your child's face.

Papaya for Smoother Skin

Do you know that kids and young adults desire smooth skin? Exfoliatingdead skin cells can assist,and papaya can act like a typical exfoliator for kidsand young adults! The energetic ingredient in papaya is papain, an enzyme that eliminates dead surface cells that give skin a matte, rugged look. Try thisfruity facial on your kids and young adultsto relax, soften, and polish their skin:

- Wash and peel ripe papaya.

- Then put two teaspoons in a food processor; blend thoroughly.

- Add one teaspoon ofwithered oatmeal; mix into a paste.

- Then apply to your freshly cleansed face and leave on for 10-15minutes.

- Remove the paste with warm wateror a soaked washcloth.

You should know papaya is a great fruit to help kids and young adults with trivial breakouts on their skin. If you want to try a blender, you can dothis; blend the papaya until it is smooth, add some oatmeal, and put it on yourface. It is a natural and safe exfoliator to eliminate dead skin that can clog pores and cause breakouts.

Mustard, Egg White, and Lavender Oil forMinorBurns

Does your child or teen enjoy cooking or baking with you? If so, have some remedies prepared forthe unavoidable minor burns.

Lavender Essential Oil

Do you know Lavender essential oil relieves burnsand takes the pain away inminutes? If you put thelavender essential oil on the burn quickly, it will kill any blistering.

Egg Whites

If your kid gets a burn, instantly grab an egg, separate the yolk, and put it on the kid's skin. Be assured it will take away the burn, heal the skin, and stop hurting. Egg white is a typical marvelousremedy to treat minor burns for youor your kids. Just rub smoothly on the burn; it removes the painand will not leave any sore on the skin. Lavender oil and mustard also work.

Mustard

Slather mustard on the seared skin when there is aburn on your kid's skin. After an initial burn, the mustard will relieve the discomfort and stop hurting and blistering. No art tells us why this works perfectly, but many willing recommendations.

Remedy for Bites and Stings

Do you know that children can't go through adolescence without a few stings from wasps,bees, or insects? It will help if you know that bitesand stings canbe severe or even life-threatening tosome kids. Some are so critical that they demand medical care. If an itchy rash or dull breathing follows a sting or bite on the kid's skin, immediately get them to a doctor! For lesser bites andstings, try these homeopathic solutions:

Poison Ivy Stings

Accept it or not, onions will kill the discomfort and inflammation (in kids) connected with poisonivy stings. All you need to do is this:

- First, cut an onion inhalf and rub it on the afflicted area.

- Then wash the area with soap and clean water.

- Lastly, use a paste of clean water and sodium bicarbonateon thearea.

Bee Stings

My mother used to help us with bee stings when I was a kid using mud and sodium bicarbonate (baking soda) combined with a bit of water to form a paste. She spanked either the mudor soda onto the bee sting, and in a few minutes, the discomfortwas gone, and the bee sting was barely noticeable. There is debate over using mud because it may have other things (and can be messy), so stick with the sodium bicarbonate (baking soda).

Wasp Stings

When a wasp stings your child, you need to be fast

as you can to act quickly. First, you must apply undiluted vinegar or lemon juice to the skin with a cotton ball. It will offset the poison immediately.

Pure Essential Oils and Herbs for Headaches

Are your kids sensitive to constant headaches? Headaches can be triggered byalcohol, chocolate, cheese, and caffeinated drinks. Besides, there are many headaches (tension, vascular, hormonal, migraine and cluster).

It will help you know that growing children may have difficulty expressing their headaches. If you suspect your child has a headache, here are some typical remedies that use herbs or essential oils. Nevertheless, some headaches are tough and demand more than a cup of tea or essential oils. Ifyou think your kid's headache is severe, consult your doctor immediately.

Essential Oils

The therapeutic-grade essential oils listed below are astounding for headachesand can be used withyoung kids:

- Rosemary

- Marjoram

- Peppermint

- Eucalyptus

- Lavender

- Grapefruit

My picks are a blend of lavender and peppermint.Here's how you should usethem for your kids:

- Take three drops of lavender oil(or any of the oils above) and rubthem into the temples on theside of your kid's head.

- Take another three drops andmassage them into the back of yourkid's head (at the base of thehead behind the ears).

- Repeat this same procedure with peppermint oil. Peppermint oil willboost the strength of any oil you use.

Herbs for Headaches

Do you know that herbs also work for headaches?You may take them as capsules or as tea. For young adults, combine the tea with a bit of honey. Giving herbs to young kids is NOT advised unlessyou work with a qualified herbalist.

The following herbs are great for headaches:

- Wood betony herb: Highlybeneficial in treating headaches

- White willow bark: It works for headaches and is close to aspirin's active principle.

- Feverfew leaf: A flowering herb most noted by experts for

its usein nursing migraine headaches. It's used to treat most of thesame ailments treated by the highly embraced aspirin.

- Chamomile: Chamomile is excellent for treating nervous headaches; itcanbe used as a tea. Mix it withpassionflower for extra advantages.

CONCLUSION

Many people believe that herbal medicines can curediseases and prevent illnesses. Whether or not thisis true, some herbs areconsidered safe for children.These herbs can help your child regain strength andvitality from the inside out. They also have powerful anti-inflammatory properties, which will help with an endless list of ailments such as headaches, muscle aches, sore throats, coughs, andfever. In addition, these herbs can be used in various ways, making them easy to incorporate intoany family's daily routine.

Herbal medicine can provide multiple benefits forchildren. The first is that it will help to strengthenthe immune system, making it easier to fight off infections; this can be an essential consideration, as childhood illnesses and diseases can be prevalent. For example, common colds, flu, bronchitis, and ear infections are common.

Another benefit of herbal medicine is the

prevention of severe illnesses like cancer and stomach ulcers, which are very common in children these days compared to years ago. In addition, herbal medicine can help to protect against significant diseases by reducing inflammation and helping to combat the harmful organisms that cause them.

Mental health has many benefits, especially inchildren with autism. The use of natural remediesin children with autism has shown to be successful in improving symptoms associated with it, such ashyperactivity and anxiety. A word to parents whenusing natural medicine: make sure you take the recommended dosage as directed on the bottle/packaging;

otherwise, you may expose your child or yourself to unnecessary side effects.

One of the most frequent methods to take herbalmedication is in the form of tea or tincture, whichis how most of these remedies are taken.

made ones. This book is an excellent resource foranyone interested in using herbal remedies to better their or their child's life.

With so many different ailments and diseases affecting children, it is essentialto know what youcan do to help improve your child's health naturallywithout having side effects. Although thisbook does not provide an extensivelist of herbal remedies for children, it does explain some of thecommon ones and provides several examples. If you are interested in herbal medicine, then it is recommended that you look for additional information on the internet or in a specialized book.

BE AN HERBALIST

INTRODUCTION

Most of us have heard or seen media about herbalism at some point. What exactly is it? Is it related to medicine in any way? Is it brand-new? The answer to all of these queries is "no." Herbalism has a long and illustrious history that spans thousands of years and continues to this day.

What are the origins of herbalism? It has been saidthat this tradition began with our ancestors in Africa, who used plant materials for food and medicines. The word "herb" is derived from the Latin word "herba," meaningherb or grasses; this means that no matter how medicine evolves, herbswill always be part of it due to their historical significance.

Herbalism has been and still is one of the most important traditional medicine systems. It has thousands of years of knowledge, skills, and experience,which cannot be matched by modern scientific medicine.

It is not only as good as modern medicine, but in some cases, it can even be better. Because herbal remedies don't have severe side effects like medication, there are no chances of overdosing onthem. For example, if you are given a prescriptionfor painkillers, the possibilities are that you will beadvised to take two or three for the pain instead ofjust one. However, taking more than prescribed can cause unwanted side effects or complications with your other medications, especially if theyinteract.

Herbal medicine is less harmful than other treatments as it aims to achieve health without causing harm to your body. Nevertheless, some people experience side effects from herbal remedies, but this is much rarer thanwhen you take medication.

This book is about how you can get started with herbalism and other traditional Chinese medicines(TCM). It is a very popular practice in China anda very important one. It has been proven that TCM cures more diseases than Western Medicine because of its natural origin. However, it's not justtheherbs but also the knowledge of their correct usage. In many respects, this is what sets it apart from conventional medicine.

As a TCM practitioner, you will have to do aninitial training that will take around four years. You can't just become one overnight.

So the first step in becoming an herbalist is tocomplete this course.

After four years, you must undergo an exam basedon your training and knowledge. If you pass this, you will have a certificate known as the "Diplomaof Acupuncture and Chinese Herbology." This gives one legal rightto practice TCM in China.

One of the reasons why TCM has survived until today is because of its scientifically proven effectiveness with various diseases. The Chinese have made amazing medical discoveries. However,the key to its survival is the ability to combine science and culture. Many of this has been achievedthrough its history and the many cultural

and social practices passed down over generations.

Another reason for its success is because it advocates a holistic approach to medicine, which means that you should look after your entire body ratherthan just your health. This way, you will look after your whole self and your sickness ordisease.

Amongst all these different features of TCM, thereis one main difference between them and WesternMedicine; it gives people a choice in how they want to cure their illnesses. Western or modern medicine gives you a prescription, while TCMgives you options. The TCM practitioner will provide you with these options, and it is your decision on what treatment method is best for you. These include traditional medicinal herbs, acupuncture, massage, and lifestyle changes.

WHY YOU SHOULD BECOME ANHERBALIST

Do you love herbs, gardening, and the outdoors? Have you always wanted to do something that could help people? Have you always wanted to take care of people's health needs but didn't know how?

Herbalism is an ancient science with asurprisingly modern application.

You may not realize it, but herbalism is gaining popularity worldwide. Did you know there are now more than 400 schools of herbal medicine? Moreover, the U.S. population has seen a sharp rise in interest over the last few years. This is no coincidence; people realize that natural resources like medicinal herbs can be far more effective thanconventional medicines (especially when it comesto chronic conditions).

Herbalism has been around for centuries but has only recently gained popularity. If you're interested

in becoming an herbalist but don't know whereto start, look at the following pages. We'll show you what is involved and dispel any myths about herbalism. In other words, this will allow you to see ifherbalism is for you.

To start, let's look at the basics of herbalism.What is it?

Many people think that herbs are just plants with pretty or medicinal properties. While that's true insome cases, it's not entirely accurate. Herbs area broad group of plants that includes trees andshrubs. It also extends to include seeds, roots, andrhizomes.

What's more, these herbs can be used in several different ways. For instance, they can be used as an ingredient in food, cosmetics, or medicine. Herbs are incredibly diverse in this regard because they can provide so many different benefits. Some of the most important herbs are also among the simplest.

Just a handful of these simple herbs include ginger,

garlic, and peppermint. These are widespread

plants, but they can do much more than spice up your dishes. They can also treat everything from indigestion to migraine pain.

While that's not even close to all these plants can do, it's an intriguing starting point for people just starting with herbalism.

What are some of the benefits of becoming an herbalist?

If you're curious about what it's like to be an herbalist, look at the following list. However, we should note that this list isn't meant to be comprehensive. After all, there are plenty of benefits associated with being an herbalist. It's also important to note that these benefits are tied with natural remedies in general, so many of them don't apply to just herbalists. These include:

- Reduced side effects: Many people prefer natural remedies over conventional ones because they offer fewer side effects. While traditional medicines can provide effective treatment for many conditions, they can also become uncomfortable or cause dangerous side effects. That's why many people choose natural remedies over conventional ones for ailments like headaches, colds, and allergies.

- Reduced expenditures: Conventional medicines can be costly if you have a chronic medical condition. After all, many of these medicines need to be taken every day. With that in mind, your medical costs can add up fast if you don't have good insurance. The average American household spends more than a third of their income on medical expenses! That's why natural alternatives like herbal remedies are so popular; they require fewer (if any) refillsand tend to cost less overall.

- Reduced chemicals: Many peopledislike the idea of their food

- being lacedwith chemicals. That's why there's been massive popularity for "all-natural"alternatives like herbal remedies. Unfortunately, the longer an herb isexposed to a chemical, the morelikely itis to become damaged or toxic. In contrast, natural herbs have only minimal exposure to these chemicals. That means they can provide all their benefits without adverse side effects.

- More natural: In many cases, you'll be able to use organic substitutes for conventional medicines. Since these are much closer to their natural forms, they tend to be more effective for various medical conditions. Even better, many of them can treat those same conditions at a much lower cost.

- Better health: Beyond conventional treatments' costs and side effects, the most significant benefit is just beinghealthier. In contrast to traditional medicines, herbal remedies don't

- contain harmful side effects. They also allow you to easily manage chronic medical conditions (like allergies). As a result, allergy sufferers need to addresstheir symptoms as soon as possible rather than waiting until it's too late.

Continue reading if you want to understandmore about herbalism.

What qualities do you possess that make you a suitable herbalist candidate? Ifyou're serious aboutbecoming an herbalist, we recommend you learn about the industry. Taking herbal classes is the most excellent method to do this. These courses will allow you to understand what it truly means tobe an herbalist. That not only affects how people view you but how your career willgo as well. For instance, if someone describes themselves as "a herbologist" or "an herbalist" and they don't studyherbs, it's easy for others to become confused. This confusion can make it harder for you to startthe industry.

That is why you must obtain a degree to work professionally as an herbalist. Degrees offered by Trinity College (for those in Ireland) or PennFoster College (for those in the United States) allow students to have the credentials they need tobecome herbalists. While a degree is not required,it can significantly improve your hiring odds.

However, if you aren't interested in working as an herbalist professionally, that doesn't mean you're out of luck! On the contrary, you shouldinvestigate herbalism for numerous reasons. Afterall, it's something that can benefit many people. You'll discover this when you explore the benefitsof herbal remedies for yourself.

HOW MUCH DO YOU LOVEHERBS?

Do you remember your family members offering you a nice warm cupof herb tea as a child? Perhapsyou had a grandmother or a loving mom who usedherb tea as a medicine when you were sick asa child.

If so, do you remember those earlier days ashealthy ones—days where all your friends were absent from school, sick with colds and flu, but not you? You were there at school no matter whatand healthy.

If you remained healthy while others were sick, you realized that your mother's or Grandma's "potions" somehow worked to boost your immunity. Of course, sometimes those cups of teadidn't taste so good, but they worked.

Maybe you had a father who loved gardening andhad a special plot reserved just for herbs. Every time you passed that section of the backyard, youhad to stop and smell the beautiful scents that interested you.

You may have thought, "One day, I will have my garden. One day I willknow how to use these herbs in cooking and what to do with them to improvehealth."

Or maybe you came from a family or a professionthat depended on medical treatments for everything from a cold to cancer, and you saw that sometimes, medical treatment wasn't helping.

You wanted something more—something thatbrought about a bit of security about getting betterand recovering—without any side effects. So you thought to yourself, "I know there must be something out there that works and can helpmama and all of us get better. One day I will find it."

You thought that if you could find out more about herbs, you could potentially gain control over your health and the health of your family.

That thought is a true statement.

The more you know and understand about

herbs, the more successful youwill be when usingthem. And the more you use herbs, the healthier you will get.

Learning About Herbs Is a Life-Changing Journey

No matter why you are interested in herbs, the good news is that you canlearn how to use herbs for healing. To do this best, becoming a Master Herbalist is the route you'll want to take.

A Master Herbalist has studied herbs—their history, how they are used, what they look like, when they are used, when they can't be used,what theirdosage is, how they grow, and how to make herbal preparations out of them.

A Master Herbalist uses herbs for all those little situations that come up at home, such as:

- What to do when you're constipated or have diarrhea.

- What to recommend when a friend or family memberhas a healthissue.

- What herbs to use when making soaps for different pleasant scents.

- How to deodorize a room from bad tobacco smokeafter a party youthrew.

- How to make herbal toothpaste when you run out of regulartoothpaste.

- How to awaken tired feet.

- What does the baby need to stop crying?

- What dad needs to do to pull down his cholesterol level.

- What aunt Sue needs to stop her PMS.

- What plants can keep away the bugs?

- What plants to eat when there's a disaster.

- What herbs can help you feel calmer or intellectually stimulated?

And a lot more!

Learning to Be a Master Herbalist Improves theQuality of Your Life

From this list, you can see that a Master Herbalist has a lot of generalknowledge on how to increase the quality of life of a person or a family. All kinds of little problems nag at us daily until we do something about them.

And often, there aren't very many options for what to do to eliminate them. Before long, we carry far too many "problems" with us through life. Then weget cranky.

Imagine on your worst day:

- Your sister had PMS.

- Your father was constipated.

- Your brother had diarrhea.

- The baby wouldn't stop crying and wouldn't go to sleep.

- Ants were marching in a line throughout your kitchento get to thesink.

- Your cousin was over and needed help while studying.

- Your feet were so tired and painful you couldn't stand.

- And you were coming down with the flu.

What would you do?

Would you know what to do to get results and have everyone smiling again?

The problem is that most people live their entire lives with these "worstdays." Their health problems keep adding up, and the years go by. People look like they've carried the world's weight—and they have!

Small Signs Become Big Health Problems

The sad part is that these issues that come up during the worst days are signs of new health problems—sometimes more severe—to show up later in life.

That PMS could be an early sign of endometriosisthat interferes with fertility. That case of constipation could become long-term and lead to colon cancer. That diarrhea could signify a parasitic infection that causes all health problems.That baby who won't go to sleep will end up disrupting your sleep and make you prone toaccidents. Rodents could soon follow those ants.

That cousin with studying problems could be diagnosed with attention deficit disorder and on Ritalin for ten years. The tired feet you feel could signify plantar fasciitis, heel spur or bunions, or other foot disorders that arise from flat feet. And that case of the flu could end up with one that hascomplications, such as diabetes or arthritis.

We must solve these little problems in our own lives. And popping a pill only creates a biggerproblem for us later, in many cases.

One of the reasons why I love being a Master Herbalist is that I love solving problems. When I do, I can stay calm no matter what happens. I always havea plan. A Master Herbalist knows howto use plants for thousands of differentsituations.

LEARNING TO HANDLE HERBS

Collecting, drying, and storing medicinal plantsare treatments thatmust be done correctly andaccurately to maintain their properties perfectly. Therefore, we discover in clear steps how toproceed with collecting, drying, and storing mostof the wild medicinal plants commonlyfound inthe American territory and many of those thatcan be grown athome. It is better to abstain from collecting medicinal herbs whenever youhave theslightest uncertainty of knowledge about it andwithout having theopportunity to ask a competentperson. In these cases, it is good practice tobuydrugs in herbal medicine shops because there are no perfect ones. Thiswill ensure that you do notmake unpleasant mistakes, and the advice of an expert can further help with treatment.

Where and How to Collect Medicinal Plants

As always, when working with plants, it is essential to proceed with method and care, both to prevent them from dying, causing damage to the environment, and for ourselves because incorrect harvesting prevents the plant from helping us again in the future. It is also essential to choose where to cultivate or harvest the medicinal herbs we need; the plants absorb everything, so we must avoid gathering those present on the roadside or near drains or intensively cultivated fields. Unfortunately, the countryside is no longer synonymous with an uncontaminated environment; it is better to look for medicinal plants in the mountains, woods, and meadows. You must find large open spaces in the plains that are not cultivated, or if they are, the cultivation methods must be traditional. Even natural watercourses are unfortunately to be avoided; in artificial canals, you have to ensure that they are only "outlets" (i.e., they do not collect water from other watercourses but only supply it). Artificial groves (poplars planted in rows used for paper and wood derivatives) are a suitable place to look for medicinal plants in the countryside.

It is necessary to have as many precautions in how we intervene on the plant and transport the harvested parts to the house; let's behave as "guests" and then interfere with moderation and cleanliness. We absolutely must not tear whole pieces of the plant with our hands but collect only the parts of our interest in the quantity we need; we will need a small knife or a shear to collect the leaves, flowers, or fruits. Even the roots must be contained in moderation. We can only take a part of them with the help of a hoe; without uprootingthe plant with our bare hands but removing it from the ground witha lot of soil around it, take some roots and replant it; in this way, the plant will continue to live, and we can use it again in thefuture. We avoid collecting protected species. Herbs, roots, flowers, and fruits should be placedin a basket covered with a light canvas fabric(allowing air to pass through), avoiding crushing

and plastic material altogether. In brief, considerthe following steps.

- Meadows bordering large cities and roadsides should be avoided, whether the latter are very busy or few cars pass by. Likewise,avoid areas close to factories and industries.

- It is good to go to the open countryside where the air is healthier, and the land is nottoo polluting if it does not contain intensivecrops.

- It is advisable to harvest the medicinal herbsin their optimal moment, called "balsamic time," which corresponds to the best evolutionary moment of the plant when its active principles are more concentrated andeffective.

- In addition, it is better for the moon to be inthe waning phase and possibly never full. Plants need a lot of sunlight and a little moonto conserve the maximum of their therapeutic virtues.

- Harvesting must take place in clear weather.Therefore,
  especially for the flowers, leaves,and fruits, i.e., the aerial
  parts of the plant, itis best to harvest in the morning, as soon
  asthe sun has dried the dew, while for the roots, the most
  suitable time is the eveningbefore sunset.

Harvest in the "Balsamic" Period

The harvest must be carried out in the period defined as "balsamic,"
which varies from plant to plant and area depending on the habitat,
climate, and the extraordinary conditions to which theplant can be
exposed. The botanical sheets you will find in the second part of the
book are therefore considered "indicative": they give general
information about the collection, but it willbe your responsibility to
evaluate the real condition of the plant before proceeding. However,
some indications cannot be omitted to have an optimal result. For
example, harvesting should be done in the morning, especially
concerning the aerial parts of the plant (everythingabove ground), not
too early: you have to wait until all the dew formed at night has dried;
otherwise, if still wet, flowers and leaves are ruinedquickly. The collection
of the roots, instead, mustbe done after rain.

Here are some indications to follow (unless otherwise indicated on the
botanical sheets) to collect the various parts of the plant at the right time:

- Seeds: When the fruit is fully ripe before it has fallenfrom
  the tree;

- Flowers: When in full bloom, before they wither;

- Leaves: Before the flowering of the plant;

- Fruits: When fully ripe;

- Stems and other parts of the plant: Collect them with flowersduring or before flowering.

- Buds: Before opening, at the beginning of spring

- Bark: Should be harvested in spring, but not on young plants.

All harvesting operations should be carried out inmoderation, without abusing a plant to prevent it from dying or ceasing to be helpful in the future.

Dry and Store Harvested Plants

Drying should be done immediately after harvesting, as soon as possible, to prevent the partfrom spoiling or starting to form bacteria away from the sun in a dry and ventilated place. The tools we use are also essential; you have to spreadthe parts of interest on trellises or wooden planks covered with a cloth that allows the air to breatheand any insects to leave the part; do not try to

"clean" the parts manually. These little guests will go on their own if youhave arranged the parts to be adequately dried. Do not use absorbent paper or plastic; the canvas must be coarse weaveand not absorb the plant's juices; it must dry in theair. Do not wash any airborne parts of the plant before or afterdrying. Drying lasts 15 to 20 days and requires maintenance: you must turn the grasses from time to time and select them bythrowing away the black parts or any mold or insects that have not left the plant. They can be stored in a glass, clay pot, paper, or canvas bag when completely dry. They must be used within ayear.

The roots and fleshy fruits should be treated differently: the roots in particular(and only those) should be washed thoroughly before proceeding. Next, both roots and fruits should be cut into thinslices and strung with a thin string, being careful that air passes between one slice and another; the drying will bedone in fresh air and sun, simply by changing the string on a sunny and ventilated spot.The drying process lasts until the roots and fruits reach a rubbery consistency; then, they must be removed from the string and storedin paper or canvas bags. To summarize:

- The flowers and leaves must be dried in the shortest possible time, put on large wicker baskets, and placed in well-ventilated and shaded rooms; attics, porches, and barns are ideal places. They are considered dry when, by touching them, they break easily.

- We use the sun or the oven at a very low temperature for the seeds, roots, and barks to open the door, so the air circulates freely. Before being exposed to the sun, the roots must be washed quickly and thoroughly, then cut into washers or strips.

- The fruits dry well exposed to the sun without previous washing. In the past, it was usedto slip them into strings in the countryside, forming longnecklaces stretched out in the sun.

NATIVE AMERICANS AND THEIR RELATIONSHIP WITH NATURE

Native Americans, also known as First Nation individuals, have used herbal medicine since the inception of their culture. This is becauseit helped to heal their body, purify their mind and evensettle their souls. However, many herbs were effective for different conditions, and the only waythey could know whether these herbs worked was to test them on animals to see the results and consequences.

North Americans did not know how to documenttheir findings then, so all herbal remedies were passed on from one person to the other via word of mouth. However, this all changed when they came in contact with the Europeans with who theyshared their findings.

This was then documented, combined with European medicine, and introduced to modernmedicine; this was great and worked fine until they decided to replace herbs with drugs just as it was in Europe. Native Americans have used theseherbs to cure some complicated medical conditions and mentally maintain a high level of balance.

Since there were different tribes in NativeAmerica, every tribe made their treatments based on their herbs. This means that other herbs were used for treating the same condition based on availability.

Native American herbal medicine did not becomethis popular because it wasperfect. Without any complications like modern medicine, No. Instead,it became popular because it got them through difficult times. Most Native American herbs are easy to track down and prevalent in specific locations in North America, and we will be looking at some of these facts in this guide.

When to Use Native American Herbs

Every situation that requires Native American herbs is different, and every human responds differently to these herbs. However, some tips areessentialto recognize when herbal medicine is a better option than the usual medical care we are used to.

As a preventive measure, one point of herbalmedicine is that it nurtures the body on a cellular level. This produces strong adaptogens, which generally increase the body's capacity to cope withthe changes that come with the surroundings andlife.

Herbs also improve the immune system functions and work almostinstantaneously for medical emergencies before reaching the hospital.For certain health conditions and auto-immune diseases like multiple sclerosis, cancer, and even AIDS, herbs help keep the body healthy, encouraging proper functionality of organs, and giving you a chance to live life to the fullest even with these conditions.

You need to know that North American herbs andmodern medicine work well together to improve the effects each one has on the body.

However, we know that medical science helps restore and enhance immune functions, which is why combining both factors is highly contemplated.

On the other hand, herbal medicine improves immune functions withoutupsetting the way you feel, and this is one of the reasons it is dubbed as oneof the most stable ways to improve health.

Numerous reports have surfaced on concerns about how good herbaceous plants are for health,with many herbs being blacklisted and termed as toxic; this is not because people use herbs but because they use them in the wrong way.

Most herbal medicines today are in capsules but inhigher doses than people usually consume when taken in as herbs, which is why people consume more than they often should.

Irrespective of how infrequent these cases of complications are with herbal remedies, one of thebest things to do is make sure you take them in recommended quantities.

Benefits and Uses of Herbal Medicine

In the United States, herbal remedies are used by millions of people for many different reasons, including to ease pain and prevent disease. In addition, herbal medicine is often used in conjunction with conventional treatment for painrelief and emotional support in the form of anxietyand stress reduction. There are many tips on using herbal medicines effectively and safely.

People have used herbal medicines since ancient times, but modern science only recentlydiscovered their benefits. For example, herbs can help ease pain by reducing inflammation or stimulating the body's natural ability to reduce swelling or release endorphins into the bloodstream. In addition, it has been proven that certain herbs can also stimulate the liver and kidneys to remove toxins from the body.

Many people have questions about herbal remedies and their benefits, both toprevent and cure disease, as well as for general health maintenance. Herbs have been used for thousands of years, but modern science still studies their effects. As a result, many misconceptions about herbal remedies today exist because of a lack of understanding of herbals and their benefits.

Herbal Medicine Benefits and Some ConditionsHelped With Herbal Remedies

Herbal medicine is used to treat conditions affecting virtually all areas of the body. There is a multitude of studies that show the benefits of using herbs to treat certain diseases or conditions.It's worth noting that not all herbs or herbal medicines have been thoroughly researched inclinical trials. However, several herbs have been demonstrated to help people with high blood pressure, diabetes, asthma, and allergies control and treat their symptoms.

Herbal medicine can help relieve pain for both acute and chronic conditions. The following herbal remedies may be used for various conditions, from pain relief to winning the war against cancer.

- Arnica montana: A popular herbused for muscle and joint pain from overuse or injury, this plantstimulates the blood flow to affected areas, promoting healing.

- Artemisia vulgaris: This herb treats coughing, bronchitis, and asthma. It has been shown to stop coughing by increasing mucus production in the respiratory system. It also helpsrelieve watery eyes, congestion in the sinuses, and headaches.

- Astragalus membranaceous: This Chinese herb has been usedfor thousands of years to improveimmune system function and enhance energy levels to help liverfunction and stimulate immunity.

- Avena sativa: This herb has long been used to treat insomnia and anxiety and decrease stress. Its calming effect helps to relax withoutcausing drowsiness.

- Boswellia serrata: This herb isbelieved to work by reducing inflammation and increasingcirculation simultaneously, thus relieving pain caused by overuseor injury. It has also been shownto slow the progression of osteoarthritis and rheumatoidarthritis.

- Bromelain: This enzyme comes from pineapple and has been shown to reduce swelling andrelieve pain.

- Capsicum frutescens: This herb contains capsaicin, which has been proven to kill cancer cells. Capsicum can be used in conjunction with chemotherapy for cancer treatment. The herb also reduces pain without the useof any medication.

- Cayenne: This red pepper treats many pain types, including muscle aches and arthritis pain. It may also help prevent heart disease as well as fight cancer. Cayenne can be taken in capsule form or applied topically over affected areas to relieve discomfort.

- Curcumin: This herb is found in the root of turmeric. It works by reducing pain, swelling, and inflammation. It is also known to fight tumors, including breast and leukemia cancer cells. In addition, this herb has shown to be effective in treating rheumatoid arthritis.

- Eucalyptus: This natural anti- inflammatory reduces swelling and inflammation of the airways and opens up the bronchial passages for easier breathing. It can be used with inhalers for asthma relief and sore throat lozenges to relieve coughs due to colds or flu.

- Ginkgo Biloba: This herb has been used for many years as an anti-inflammatory and to promote circulation. It is believed to increase blood circulation by helping the body remove toxins in tissue.

- Ginger: This herb simultaneously reduces pain by stimulating circulation and digestion. It can be taken as a capsule or used topically for

immediate pain relief. It can alsobe used to relieve nausea, vomiting, and indigestion. Ginger may also control intestinal spasms and possess antibacterial activity that kills harmful varieties such as Salmonella, E. coli, and theH1N1 virus (swineflu).

- Ginseng: This herb stimulates the immune system, enhances energy, decreases fatigue, and improves the appearance of skin. It may also help people with diabetes control their blood sugar levels and prevent liver damage. In addition, ginseng, especially ginseng root, is believed to help alleviate pain caused by arthritis and rheumatism.

- Kava: Kava has been used as ananxiolytic for thousands of years, meaning it calms anxiety by relaxing muscles while enhancing mental alertness. Kava appears to have the reverse effect of relaxing nerves, increasing anxiety levels and causing tiredness or dizziness in some persons who use it.

- Licorice: This herb has been used for decades because of its abilityto relieve pain and reduce inflammation. It may also have anti-viral and antibacterial properties. In addition, it may help the body resist viruses and bacterial infections.

- Melissa officinalis: This herb is a good source of vitamins A, C, D, and E, as well as thiamine, riboflavin, and niacin. In addition, it has been shown to modulate symptoms of Alzheimer's disease.

- Mind-Altering Herbs: This category is where you will find several herbs used for centuries by indigenous peoples of the world.These mind-altering herbs include ayahuasca, cannabis, ephedra, iboga, d-lysergic acid diethylamide (LSD), peyote, and San Pedro cactus.

- Motherwort: This herb has a long history of use as a medicine for PMS symptoms and anxiety. It is also believed to reduce pain caused by heartburn and arthritis in the spine. In addition, it is similar to valerian root and may help naturally regulate brain functions and sleep cycles.

- MSM: This is one of the most affordable and effective anti-inflammatory agents. MSMworks by reducing inflammationand swelling caused by injuries, arthritis, tendinitis, and evenback pain. Nettle: This herb has been used for its numerous benefits for generations. It is a natural diuretic that helps reduce swelling in the body caused by fluid retention. It also improves digestion by stimulating acidsecretion in the stomach toprevent heartburn and indigestion by decreasing abdominal bloating and pain. Nettle helpsto detoxify the liver and increase circulation. It is alsoa good sourceof B vitamins and iron. It has pain-relieving properties, including anti-inflammatory and anti-spasmodic actions that may alleviate joint pain and muscle aches. This plant can be used in capsule or teaform.

- Panax ginseng: Ginseng extractshave been used for thousands of years to reduce pain, improvecirculation, maintain healthybreathing passages, and increaseoverall energy production for mental and physical health.

- Passionflower: This herb is usedfor headaches, insomnia, and muscle soreness. It works by reducing sweating, reducing pain, and inhibiting muscle spasms. Passionflower is also used to treat anxiety, such as post-traumatic stress disorder.

- Peppermint: Peppermint hasbeen used to relieve gastricdiscomfort associated with heartburn and nausea caused by motion sickness, morning sickness, or pregnancy. It can be used in conjunction with inhalers to treat osteoarthritis, rheumatoid arthritis,and asthma because of its ability to reduce inflammation and swelling.

- Red Clover: This herb is frequently used to treat menopausal symptoms such as hot flashes, night sweats, and restlessness in the legs at night. It also helps to reduce inflammation and swelling caused by injuries, arthritis, tendonitis, and asthma.

- Rosemary: Rosemary works by stimulating the brain and nervous system to improve concentration and mental alertness and increase energy levels for psychological and physical health. It is believed to help reduce pain caused by muscle aches or joint pain. It canbe taken as a pill or used topically for rapid relief from chronic or acutepain.

- Rosehips: Rosehips are the seed clusters of the rose. It is an excellent source of vitamin C,potassium, and beta-carotene. Rosehip oil is sometimes used totreat minor wounds, bruises, andburns. It can also help digestion and act as an immunity booster for vitamin C deficient persons.

- Sage: This herb has been used asa natural antibacterial and musclerelaxant for ages. It helps reduceinflammation and promotes circulation throughout the body.It also helps regulate body functions and has a calming effect. It may help people who experience anxiety, tension, milddepression, or mood swings.

- Siberian Ginseng: Siberian ginseng is believed to promote longevity and increase energy levels for both mental and physical health. It is used for anemia, angina pectoris, arthritis, cardiovascular disease, and rheumatism or sore muscles.It also assists persons who arevitamin C deficient in maintaining their immunesystems. Siberian ginseng can be either a capsule or a tea.

- St. John's Wort: This herb has beenused to treat depression and anxiety. It relieves inflammation of the eyes, mouth, throat, and digestive tract, as well as rheumatism and aching muscles, thanks toits capacity to reduce inflammation and swelling.

- Vitamins A and Cand magnesium,manganese, and copper are abundant in St. John's Wort.

- Turmeric: This plant is well- known for its anti-inflammatory properties, which help to alleviate joint and muscular symptoms caused by arthritis or muscle injuries. It can also help with asthma, rheumatoidarthritis, and ulcerative colitis. Itis believed to help regulate the body's natural inflammatory response and boost immunity. Inaddition, turmeric may help to lower cholesterol levels and reduce the risk of heart disease by preventing blood clots from forming.

- Valerian root: This herb has been used for centuries to reduce anxiety and promote relaxation. It is believed to work by slowing down the activity of certain neurons in the brain that control over- stimulation and excitability in areas responsible for tension, agitation, insomnia, and irritability. It also increases cerebral blood flow, improving oxygenation to the brain and central nervous system. It's available as a capsule or a tea.

- Wild Yam: This herb is used for menstrual symptoms and menopause, and irregular periods. It is believed to reduce PMS- related irritability, anxiety, and sweating, particularly with period- related cramps. In addition, this herb has been used to help relieve symptoms of menopause such as hot flashes, night sweats, and rheumatoid arthritis.

The best times to take these supplements arewhen you awaken in the morning and beforeyou go to bed at night. Another good time isto take these supplements before lunch. By taking a variety of these supplements daily, you'll be well-nourished and will feel great!

Bottom Line

Native America is one of the birthplaces of herbalmedicine, and their relationship with nature was strong enough to make them understand the benefits of certain herbal medicines. This connection has been translated to many locationstoday, making it great for being used by many people.

Dried Simples

Simply put, dried herbs used in teas (also known as tisanes, a lovely French term) are also referred to as infusions or decoctions.

The distinction in both terms is the volume of dry plant content compared to the amount of water used and the length of time it is steeped or simmered. It is not to be confused with black tea, such as Darjeeling or oolong, which has its cult.

Aluminum and iron can never be used to make medicinal remedies since they negatively affect the plants.

Instead, cook your brews with stainless steel, enamelware, or heat-tempered glass, and use good water. If you have chlorinated municipal water, you may want to invest in a water filter for your daily drinking water.

Herb Tea

Use one rounded teaspoon (not exactly a measuring teaspoon, but the sortyou stir with) dried, crushed plant material or two teaspoons fresh to a teacup or mug full of boiling water for abasic herbal beverage, or tisane, steeping (soaking)for just a few minutes.

To make it simpler to strain, soak in a jar (or teapot—hey, there's an idea!), then spill into the cup and sweeten if necessary. While most teas arediuretic to a degree, two or three cups a day is notexcessive.

Tea can be made from various spices, such as spearmint, chamomile, or nettles, and it's pleasantto try different flavor variations.

Herbal Infusion

A strong tea used as a medicine is known as an herbalinfusion. Add one ounce of dry plant material (usually leaves or flowers) to one pint of boiling water, cover, and steep for ten to fifteen minutes. The herb is not cooked either way.

Remove the filter and serve. This is the herbal teadosage, and depending on the cure, you can only take a couple of sips at a time. Some guidelines specify whether to drink hot or cold and the righttime of day.

Herbal Decoction

Use one-ounce dry plant content (usually a harderpart of the plant, such as the base, bark, twig, seed,or berry) to one-pint water for a decoction. This excellent herbal tea is simmered, then cover and boil for around fifteenminutes, depending on the plant parts and desired weight. In realistic terms, an ounce of dry plant content will hold up to a cupof liquid.

Herbal Poultice or Plaster

Using moisture and heat aids the curing operation

of this process of using herbs. In addition, they treat wounds, minimize pain, break up congestion,and function as a sliver or infection- drawing agent.

Simple Poultice

Fresh herbs such as chickweed, self-heal (heal-all),violet leaf, or other gentleemollient herbs may be mashed up in a bowl with a fork or a wooden spoon, buzzed in a blender, or chewed into a pulp(this is particularly useful out on the trail) and applied directly to the infected region is one way to create a poultice—the simplest way, in truth.

The poultice is held with a slice of cabbage, plantain, or another broad, non- irritating leaftightly protected with a strip of gauze ribbon.

Alternatively, you should stay still for a couple of minutes while the poultice does its magic and thengo about your business. Chickweed (Stellaria media),a native garden "weed," may be used to treat contaminated splinters.

Compound Plaster

Another kind of poultice, or plaster, is produced by grinding the desired driedherb and combining it with an equivalent amount of bran, oatmeal, orflaxseed meal (or another neutral medium) with only enough boiling water to create a wet paste.

The quantities required are determined by theregion's size to be covered. First, cover with a soft, moistened piece of muslin or cheesecloth designed to fit the infected area, then cover with adry cloth. A typical Chinese treatment forpulmonary problems (chest), kidney blockage (middle back), and menstrual cramps is a ginger compress (abdomen and lower back).

The herbal plaster is less common than a plain poultice or herb compress, partly because it is more expensive and somewhat because it is challenging to spread on one's own. Some plasters, such as apple plaster for sunburn, maybe produced without the bran and just the plant content.

Herb Compress

A compress is equivalent to plaster, but it is oftenless complicated. A solid, hot infusion of the herbof choice is produced.

Dip soft cloths or towels in the tea, wring them out, then apply to the infectedregion. Cover the "user" with a towel or blanket to keep them covered.

Any compresses, such as those for sunburn or sprains, can be excellent. But, of course, specific cases, such as a fractured bone, will need cold applications, at least before immediate medicalhelp arrives; we must use justification and common sense while handling ourselves, and understanding our limits is part of it.

Herbal Tinctures

A way of concentrating the therapeutic propertiesof herbs for internal usage is to make an alcohol- based tincture with fresh or dried herbs. Herbal remedies have the advantage of lasting almostindefinitely.

These are made by steeping one pint (or sufficiently liquid to cover the herb) of good- quality vodka in a new and clean jar with approximately one ounceof dried or four ounces of fresh plant content, chopped or gently crushed(do not powder).

Put the date and label. The tincture can steep for two weeks or longer if the compound is thicker. Although certain herbalists recommend brandy orgin for fresh flowers, leaves, and dried plants, we choose vodka (precisely 50% alcohol and 50% water).

For fresh roots or rugged or resinous plant stuff, such as cottonwood buds, pure grain alcohol, or Everclear, if you can't find Everclear, consider 151- proof rum.

Since tinctures are condensed, the dosage is usually given in drops (rather than droppers-full), ranging between ten to thirty drops per adult dose,depending on the herbs and the person's weight. To avoid burning yourtongue, dilute the drops in some water.

Rubbing alcohol and wood alcohol can never be internally used since theyare highly harmful once consumed. You may produce an herbal cream forexterior use with rubbing alcohol, but good old vodka is recommended.

Well, it is more costly, but it is also better. Fill small dropper bottles of your tinctures, which youcan get from your nearest pharmacy or buy online— mark all of your herbal items with the date, ingredients, and intended use.

Herbal Wine

Certain herbs may be steeped in wine—for example, May wine, made with sweet woodruff and German white wine—but these are meant to be consumed immediately since they don't keep well.

You know if they're an excellent way to take your medication or a medicinal way to enjoy. To infuse the wine with herbs, pour one bottle (1 quarter, 45 quarts, or 750 ml) of wine into a quart jar with a half cup of new, clean herbs or edible flowers, the combinations of which are only limited by your imagination.

Using dried spices like clove or cinnamon, use a few bits simultaneously because they're very potent. The elder steal, made from dried elderberries and a cinnamon stick mulled in a dry red wine like burgundy, is one example of herb- infused wine for medicinal purposes.

Infusing herbs in wine solely for flavoring purposes is perfectly acceptable.

Oil Extracts

To render soothing rubs for various uses, soak such herbs in oil.

Pure olive oil has a long shelf life and is the most often used oil for salves; almond oil makes a fine basis for special body oils.

Place one pint of oil, two ounces of dried plant content, or four ounces of fresh herbs in a small saucepan, and cover with more oil if desired.

Place the saucepan over a low heat setting and soak the herbs in the oil for many hours, stirring regularly to avoid scorching. Depending on the plant material, you will want to steep for a couple of days; in this situation, switch off the heat overnight (cover with a towel so it can evaporate)and re-start the gentle warmth in the morning.

It is primed when the oil smells fragrant and has arich color from the herbs—indeed, the herbs mayhave lost some of their green colors. After straining outthe herbs, cool the oil before placing it in a clean, dry container.

It has been discovered that a mini slow cooker is an excellent gentle warming vessel for steepingherbs in oil, especially fresh herbs since you can leave the lid off to allow the water in the plant material to evaporate and keep itrunning for a couple of days without concern.

The herbs can mold if you don't use some heat and instead soak fresh herbs and oil in a container withthe lid on. As a result, unless vinegar is used, it is no longer advisable to infuse garlic in oil at any time, as it may trigger botulism in an anaerobic (airless) atmosphere. So while you are unlikely to use herbal oil extracts, the idea remains the same.

While using fresh plants, gentle heat of any kind isrecommended. Herbal oil extracted from birch twigs or cottonwood buds produces an excellent analgesic rub that often smells great.

For bruising and muscle spasms, apply St. John's Wort spray. Make an after- shower body oil by steeping fragrant flower petals and herbs. Glass bottlesare best for storing oils.

Herbal Salves, Ointments Balms, and Unguents

These words are synonymous with treatments forsuperficial scrapes, abrasions, and various skinailments.

Some oil extracts are prepared as before and thickened or hardened with beeswax or another strong fat such as cocoa butter, coconut oil, or deer fat if you have a hunter in the home.

Lip balm is a fancy word for salve.

Make the salve with herbs that fit your needs, such as cedar leaves for antifungal properties, chickweed, plantain for emollient properties, Oregon grape leaf for infection prevention, or comfrey root for rapid healing.**Basic Salve**

Stir approximately one-ounce grated beeswax into one-pint warm oil extract prepared as directed above. You'll have to experiment with a specific thickener because it's difficult to predict how viscous the oil would be.

Scoop up a teaspoon of the oil-wax mixture and dump it onto a small plate to search for its hardness; after a few minutes, it will have cooled, and you may measure its strength. It can slosh around in the bottle if it is too smooth, and it will be impossible to get a lick out of it if it is too stiff.

Salves may be formulated from several types of oil extracts or oil extracts made from various herbs.

In addition, tiny quantities of other additives, such as honey, lanolin, or vitamin E oil, may also be added.

Put label and date. Keep your salves in thin, wide-mouthed pots, but don't cover them until they're completely cool. Look for beautiful jars to provide as gifts.

Making salves is an organic, hands-on method that can be messy sometimes, but that's just part of the fun. Children may assist in the project by identifyingand harvesting medicinal plants.

Lip Balm

Make the oil extract with one cup of almond oil and one-fourth cup of dried rose petals or calendula petals (or both) in the same way assalves; steep for many hours to overnight, and usea very gentle fire. Return to the heat, strain,and stirin around one tablespoon of grated beeswax with a chopstick to mix.

You should also try a drop or two of glycerin-

based vanilla or almondflavoring, up to a teaspoonof vitamin E oil, and a dab of honey or cocoa

butter (not to be confused with the alcohol-basedvanilla extract you might beused to).

Blend properly, and gently pour into multiple littlecontainers large enough to drop a pinky finger, leaving the lids off before the mixture cools. Lip balm created at home is a great present.

Herbal Syrups and Elixirs

Herbal syrups may treat sore throats and coughs and make sour herb tonics. Rosehips, elderberries, blackberries, violet leaf and vine, red clover blossom, and the infamous horehound can createexcellent syrups.

Of course, some herbal syrups may be used on biscuits, hot cereal, roast meatglazing, and hot beverages. When I make herbal syrups, I often use honey, which is soothing in and of itself for a sorethroat, particularly when combined with a squeezeof lemon.

Please remember that honey should not be provided to children under one year because it cancontain botulism spores, which are harmless to adults but dangerous to children.

For an "average-sized" human, one stirring spoonof syrup is usually enough;use more for bigger people and fewer for children. It is possible to takeup to eight doses a day.

Boil one quart of water with two ounces of dry orfour ounces of fresh plant content in a smallsaucepan; reduce heat to low and simmer uncovered for twenty minutes, or until decreased by half, leaving one pint.

Strain, then whisk in a half cup of honey until smooth. If you're using sugar instead of honey, useone cup of sugar and return the strained herbal decoction to medium heat until it's fully dissolved before decanting, which should just take a few minutes.

Fill sterilized bottles halfway with the hot liquid, mark, and date them. The syrup can be stored in the refrigerator for three months.

Elderberry elixir can treat flu symptoms. Comfrey

root, mullein vine, and hawthorn berries can beused as a healing expectorant, and violet flower

syrup can be applied to hot water to make adelicate drink. Rosehip syrup hasan almost apple-like flavor.

Consider a selection of minted syrups. Decanting culinary syrups into decorative bottles allows a lovely gift presentation.

TIPS ABOUT HERBALISTS

This brief text reveals a great deal about the life ofa Master Herbalist. Here's a rundown of some of the key points:

1. Friends Refer Their Friends to Herbalists

It's rare for calls to come out of the blue. This is because the people who tendto use herbs also tendto have friends who use herbs.

Usually, the people who realize that there arenatural solutions for daily life situations often have struggled with health issues themselves. However, they overcame that issue by using natural solutions such as herbs or foods, and ever since then, their minds have opened up to the possibility that otherthings could be healed from herbs.

After their healing, they become sensitive to people who don't believe in herbs. So, naturally, they begin gravitating toward people who have had similar situations in life. They crave hearing other people's stories and want to know what is possible from natural healing.

As you already know, much herbal knowledge is passed down through the ages in story format. This is one of the best ways to ensure that someone remembers it. As a memory expert for over ten years, I found that telling people stories was at least twice as effective at remembering the information as just talking about facts.

The facts about herbs are always essential, too, butthe stories give you a quick spark of wisdom whenyou're in a situation and may not know what to do.

2. <u>Ask Details Before the Client Shows Up</u>

Herbalists will always ask questions about asituation before the appointment time. This is to know what herb may be needed and ensure it is instock. Herbalists have at least one storeroom filled with various herbs that can be mixed to create a combination that the client can take for healing.In a simple telephone conversation, it wasdiscovered that the plant most likely to be used for a baby was an herb that was gentle enough for them and yet strong enough to eliminate constipation.

3. Recognizing the Severity of an Issue

With adequate herbal training, an herbalist can first decide whether or not an issue the client is facing needs to be dealt with or can wait.

For example, constipation is a backup of the body's plumbing system. Unfortunately, the backup gets worse the longer this goes on. To an herbalist,any backup in the system needs to be addressed immediately.

That's why the appointment was set up for the afternoon at the earliest time the client could comein. A backup in the colon is a setup for a backup in the liver and kidneys. Eventually, all organs willsuffer if the condition goes on for too long.

4. <u>The Client Should Be Seen in Person</u>

Herbalists could conceivably consult with clientsthey already
know via phone consultation, butseeing clients in person is always
the best idea.

For example, when Sandy brings in her baby, it ispossible to see what
else may be happening. Maybe the baby has lost all its hair from another
condition. Perhaps the baby wasn't growing at all.Maybe the baby had a
disability that needed to betaken into consideration.

None of these would have been discovered without seeing the baby
in person.However, aparent who calls on the phone may overlook these
"little" details just because the parent has been dealing with them and is
more focused on what's happening with the child.

Sometimes, the herbalists have to use common sense and tell a client to
go to the doctor. For example, a client may have exceptional abdominal
pain, a high fever that came on suddenly, or other severe medical
conditions.

Most importantly, a Master Herbalist recognizes when the client needs
additional help. This istaught in herbal training.

Referring a client to a medical doctor is not a surrender. An herbalist is
a professional that often

works with other health professionals. Knowing one's limitations is
essential.

If you wanted to buy a pair of sneakers, but the store only had dress
shoes, you'd expect the storeowner to refer you to a sneakers store. It's

the same thing with the body.

An herbalist can only do so much, although theycan do a lot. A massage therapist can only do so much with her skills, too. A chiropractor also has limitations. And even a medical doctor is worthless if the client needs a root canal!

Thus, one characteristic of a good herbalist is to know when to refer the clientand not feel wrong about the referral.

CONCLUSION

I have been practicing herbalism for several years now, and I have found thatit is gratifying. Not onlydid I win a prestigious award, my health improved,and so did my family's health. As a result, I started teaching other people about herbalism. You learned how to create an herb garden in this book. Before getting started, you need toknow some points, including how often herbs should be cut back for use or harvest and what kind of soil to prepare for your herb garden.

It is paramount to learn about herbs before you start your herb garden. The best idea is to visit your local library and read about herbs. Find out what ingredients the herbs contain and what health conditions they can treat. If youhave time, try growing one of the most common herbs in your region. You can develop a few more popularones so people can sample them when they visit your garden. You might want to keep a journal

when growing common herbs, especially if you seeresults immediately.

Once you have learned about herbs, purchase a large container. These containers range in sizefrom a large washtub to a five-gallon bucket. First,you must decide how big your herb garden is. Make it small if you only need one herb in your garden. You can have many herbs in the same container if you have time to pick and use them. I would recommend growing at least three herbs ineach container so that you can alternate which is used each week by adding it every two weeks so that the herbs will be fresher for more extended periods.

Choose where you are going to plant your herb garden. If in a city, you have the option of plantingnext to a concrete wall and creating a fence surrounding your garden. This will give your herbsmore space which is beneficial because, as a beginner, it's hard to know when not to cut back the herbs from being overgrown.

I would recommend moving the herb garden if any of these conditions apply.

- There are sprinkler heads spraying water directly on top ofthe soil.

- You do not feel safe having children nearby.

- You don't want to disturb the neighbor too much or get nailedfor having dirt escape on their lawn.

- The area does not receive fullsunlight all day.

- You don't want to move the herb garden every year because of badconditions in the location.

Now that you have chosen where you want your herb garden, you need to prepare the soil. It is bestto start with a wood chip bed, so it is easier on your back when doing other more difficult chores like digging and moving rocks around. If your areahas a lot of clay in the soil, you should consider adding sand and gravel to loosen it up. After you have added the wood chips and sand, you will want to compost twice a year. Composting keeps the soil healthy and fertilized for your herbs.

To plant your herbs, ensure the herb seeds are thoroughly cleaned before planting. Then gently rake it over with a rake to keep from getting weedsfrom your herb garden. If you don't have a rake, a sharp spade will suffice until all of the rockson both sides of the herb garden have been removed. Next, fill the holes to ensure the soil is complete and there are no rocks underneath.

You will need to decide what soil you want for your herb garden. Next, look at your herbs and choose which do best in your area. Some common herbs in my area are cilantro, rosemary, basil, thyme, mint, and chamomile. Thesefour herbs can be used for many different purposes, from being used as an herb tea to a salad garnish; even frozen into ice cubes by putting all together in a food processor with a little water and then adding2-3 ice cubes when heating or cooking somethingin your kitchen. If you want to use fresh herbs butdon't want the aftertaste of fresh herbs in your cuisine, this is a fantastic option.

If you choose to plant cilantro, basil, or mint, plantthem where they will be easy to reach when harvesting. Do not plant anything near mint if you want itto stay healthy. The oils in mint will destroyall other plants around it. It is best to put it as far away from your other plants as possible so that they are not affected by its oils. You can go into your herb garden and pull it out or spray it with asolution of water and vinegar once or twice a month to prevent any weeds from invading.

Once you have put your herbs in their containers,they will need to bewatered regularly. Before youstart watering, make sure that the herb plants are moist but not dripping wet. If the soil is too dry, you'll need to add extra soil mix before going further. Overwatering will cause the roots in the container to rot, resulting in the death of your herbs and, on the other hand, causing them to spread out and start lanky. Your plants need water,but they do not all need to be soaked. It is agood idea to get a watering can so thatyou arenot overwatering or underwatering the herbs.

Watering your herbs is quick and easy. Simply usethe hose and spray it lightly on the entire plant after clippings have been removed for use. When cutting off the top of a plant, make sure you leaveabout 3" of stem underground so that it does not die during its first month in the garden. You will notice the plants growing for about two to three weeks before it stops. If you're still having weed difficulties, consider spreading a little slug baitaround the perimeter of your garden or plant. Youmay also want to pull up any weeds that grow in the garden after a few weeks and put them in another container to continue growing for a little longer.

Leaving the leaves of your herbs is not very important because they will distract pests andinsects from the plant, and these naturally collect their nutrients while they grow, so they don't need assistance from you. However,if you choose to leave your plants, make sure that it is something they like to eat. For example, you can cut off a leaffrom a plant, pull a weed from the garden, and putit into its container with water. The plant will use the nutrients from the leaves, and it will also helpto keep your herbs healthy.

Herbs grow better if you root them in water instead of setting them out in the ground. To do this, find a glass container with holes in the bottom, fill it halfway with water with no chlorineor fluoride added, and place your herb stem into the water. You will want to change the water every two weeks to keep your herb roots fresh. Once the roots start growing, then you can takethe herbs out and plant them in your garden.

Your herbs will need to be fertilized at least three times a year. Whenfertilizing your herbs, you wantto use a shallow rake or hoe to eliminate weeds. Make sure that the soil is loose before you put in some fertilizer, and hot for your herb plants to handle.